Little Squirrel, Little Squirrel, Noisy as Can Be!

By CHARLES GHIGNA
Illustrations by ELLEN STUBBINGS
Music by ERIK KOSKINEN

CANTATA
LEARNING

WWW.CANTATALEARNING.COM

CANTATA
LEARNING

Published by Cantata Learning
1710 Roe Crest Drive
North Mankato, MN 56003
www.cantatalearning.com

A note to educators and librarians from the publisher: Cantata Learning has provided the following data to assist in book processing and suggested use of Cantata Learning product.

Publisher's Cataloging-in-Publication Data
Prepared by Librarian Consultant: Ann-Marie Begnaud
Library of Congress Control Number: 2016938055
    Little Squirrel, Little Squirrel, Noisy as Can Be!
    Series: Father Goose : Animal Rhymes
    By Charles Ghigna
    Illustrations by Ellen Stubbings
    Music by Erik Koskinen
    Summary: Children interact with animals at a nature preserve in this original rhyme set to music.
    ISBN: 978-1-63290-771-4 (library binding/CD)
Suggested Dewey and Subject Headings:
    Dewey: E 591.59
    LCSH Subject Headings: Animal sounds – Juvenile literature. | Forest animals – Juvenile literature. | Animal sounds – Songs and music – Texts. | Forest animals – Songs and music – Texts. | Animals sounds – Juvenile sound recordings. | Forest animals – Juvenile sound recordings.
    Sears Subject Headings: Animal sounds. | Forest animals. | School songbooks. | Children's songs. | Folk music – United States.
    BISAC Subject Headings: JUVENILE NONFICTION / Concepts / Sounds. | JUVENILE NONFICTION / Music / Songbooks. | JUVENILE NONFICTION / Animals / General.

Book design and art direction: Tim Palin Creative
Editorial direction: Flat Sole Studio
Music direction: Elizabeth Draper
Music written and produced by Erik Koskinen and recorded at Real Phonic Studios

Printed in the United States of America in North Mankato, Minnesota.
122016   0339CGS17

ACCESS THE MUSIC!

SCAN CODE WITH MOBILE APP

CANTATALEARNING.COM

TIPS TO SUPPORT LITERACY AT HOME

WHY READING AND SINGING WITH YOUR CHILD IS SO IMPORTANT

Daily reading with your child leads to increased academic achievement. Music and songs, specifically rhyming songs, are a fun and easy way to build early literacy and language development. Music skills correlate significantly with both phonological awareness and reading development. Singing helps build vocabulary and speech development. And reading and appreciating music together is a wonderful way to strengthen your relationship.

READ AND SING EVERY DAY!

TIPS FOR USING CANTATA LEARNING BOOKS AND SONGS DURING YOUR DAILY STORY TIME

1. As you sing and read, point out the different words on the page that rhyme. Suggest other words that rhyme.

2. Memorize simple rhymes such as Itsy Bitsy Spider and sing them together. This encourages comprehension skills and early literacy skills.

3. Use the questions in the back of each book to guide your singing and storytelling.

4. Read the included sheet music with your child while you listen to the song. How do the music notes correlate to the words of the song?

5. Sing along on the go and at home. Access music by scanning the QR code on each Cantata book, or by using the included CD. You can also stream or download the music for free to your computer, smartphone, or mobile device.

Devoting time to daily reading shows that you are available for your child. Together, you are building language, literacy, and listening skills.

Have fun reading and singing!

The children in this song visit a nature preserve. They see and hear many different animals in the forest and in the prairie. What kind of sounds does each animal make?

To find out, turn the page and sing along!

SCHOOL BUS

Little deer, little deer,
noisy as can be,
I hear you.
Can you hear me?

Yes, I hear you **dash**, passing in a flash.

Just like me, it's fun to see you dash, dash, dash!

Little squirrel, little squirrel,
noisy as can be,
I hear you.
Can you hear me?

8

Yes, I hear you **scamper** like a little champ.

Just like me, it's fun to see you scamp, scamp, scamp!

9

Little bat, little bat,
noisy as can be,
I hear you.
Can you hear me?

Yes, I hear you flap,
waking from a nap.

Just like me, it's fun to see
you flap, flap, flap!

Little bear, little bear,
noisy as can be,
I hear you.
Can you hear me?

Yes, I hear you **grunt** when you look for lunch.

Just like me, it's fun to see you grunt, grunt, grunt!

13

Little fox, little fox,
noisy as can be,
I hear you.
Can you hear me?

Yes, I hear you **yip**
as you jump and skip.

Just like me, it's fun to see
you yip, yip, yip!

17

Little wolf, little wolf,
noisy as can be,
I hear you.
Can you hear me?

Yes, I hear you howl
when you start to prowl.

Just like me, it's fun to see
you howl, howl, howl!

19

Little crow, little crow,
noisy as can be,
I hear you.
Can you hear me?

Yes, I hear you **caw**
in a field of straw.

Just like me, it's fun to see
you caw, caw, caw!

SONG LYRICS
Little Squirrel, Little Squirrel, Noisy as Can Be!

Little deer, little deer,
noisy as can be,
I hear you.
Can you hear me?

Yes, I hear you dash,
passing in a flash.
Just like me, it's fun to see
you dash, dash, dash!

Little squirrel, little squirrel,
noisy as can be,
I hear you.
Can you hear me?

Yes, I hear you scamper
like a little champ.
Just like me, it's fun to see
you scamp, scamp, scamp!

Little bat, little bat,
noisy as can be,
I hear you.
Can you hear me?

Yes, I hear you flap,
waking from a nap.
Just like me, it's fun to see
you flap, flap, flap!

Little bear, little bear,
noisy as can be,
I hear you.
Can you hear me?

Yes, I hear you grunt
when you look for lunch.
Just like me, it's fun to see
you grunt, grunt, grunt!

Little fox, little fox,
noisy as can be,
I hear you.
Can you hear me?

Yes, I hear you yip
as you jump and skip.
Just like me, it's fun to see
you yip, yip, yip!

Little wolf, little wolf,
noisy as can be,
I hear you.
Can you hear me?

Yes, I hear you howl
when you start to prowl.
Just like me, it's fun to see
you howl, howl, howl!

Little crow, little crow,
noisy as can be,
I hear you.
Can you hear me?

Yes, I hear you caw
in a field of straw.
Just like me, it's fun to see
you caw, caw, caw!

Little Squirrel, Little Squirrel, Noisy as Can Be!

Pop
Erik Koskinen

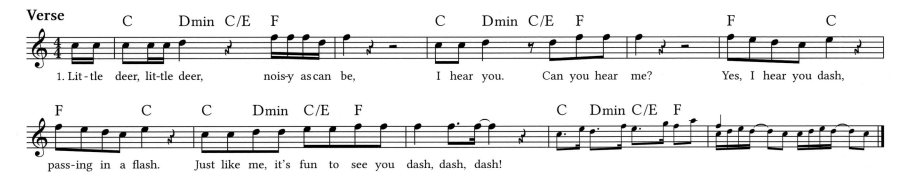

Verse

1. Lit-tle deer, lit-tle deer, nois-y as can be, I hear you. Can you hear me? Yes, I hear you dash, pass-ing in a flash. Just like me, it's fun to see you dash, dash, dash!

Verse 2
Little squirrel, little squirrel,
noisy as can be,
I hear you.
Can you hear me?
Yes, I hear you scamper
like a little champ.
Just like me, it's fun to see
you scamp, scamp, scamp!

Verse 3
Little bat, little bat,
noisy as can be,
I hear you.
Can you hear me?
Yes, I hear you flap,
waking from a nap.
Just like me, it's fun to see
you flap, flap, flap!

Verse 4
Little bear, little bear,
noisy as can be,
I hear you.
Can you hear me?
Yes, I hear you grunt
when you look for lunch.
Just like me, it's fun to see
you grunt, grunt, grunt!

[musical break]

Verse 5
Little fox, little fox,
noisy as can be,
I hear you.
Can you hear me?
Yes, I hear you yip
as you jump and skip.
Just like me, it's fun to see
you yip, yip, yip!

Verse 6
Little wolf, little wolf,
noisy as can be,
I hear you.
Can you hear me?
Yes, I hear you howl
when you start to prowl.
Just like me, it's fun to see
you howl, howl, howl!

Verse 7
Little crow, little crow,
noisy as can be,
I hear you.
Can you hear me?
Yes, I hear you caw
in a field of straw.
Just like me, it's fun to see
you caw, caw, caw!

GLOSSARY

caw—the harsh cry of a crow or other bird

dash—to move with sudden speed

grunt—a deep, short sound made by an animal

scamper—to run lightly and playfully about

yip—a short, sharp cry

GUIDED READING ACTIVITIES

1. Name some of the animals in this book. Which one is your favorite? Draw a picture of your favorite animal from this book.

2. The animals in this book make lots of different sounds. Can you caw like a crow? Can you grunt like a bear? What sound does a wolf make?

3. Would you like to go on a field trip to the nature preserve? Why or why not? Which animals would you hope to see.

TO LEARN MORE

Anderson, Steven. *Home on the Range*. North Mankato, MN: Cantata Learning, 2016.

Dahl, Michael. *Wolves*. North Mankato, MN: Capstone, 2012.

Kolpin, Molly. *Grizzly Bears*. North Mankato, MN: Capstone, 2013.

Schuh, Mari. *Squirrels*. North Mankato, MN: Capstone, 2015.